INDIGENOUS AMERICAN CULTURES

Celebrating the ABENAKI

KIM THOMPSON

Mitchell Lane
PUBLISHERS

Parent and Caregiver Tips for Creating Nonfiction Readers

The high-interest topics in the ***Indigenous American Cultures*** series are sure to get your young reader excited about reading nonfiction. While exploring a fascinating subject, your reader will be introduced to new facts, ideas, and vocabulary.

Tips for Reading Nonfiction

Talk about Nonfiction

Explain that nonfiction books provide facts about real-world topics. When readers read nonfiction, they gain a rich understanding of the world. They build background knowledge that provides a foundation for learning and academic success.

Look at the Parts

This book contains the following helpful features. Share the purpose of each feature with your reader.

Photos, Captions, and Graphic Aids
The photos, captions, maps, diagrams, time lines, and other graphic aids in nonfiction texts contain a wealth of information. Help your reader identify different ways information can be displayed.

Sidebars
These extra tidbits of information help satisfy readers' curiosity and expand their knowledge.

Table of Contents
Located at the front of the book, this list shows the big ideas within the text and the page numbers where they can be found.

Glossary
Located at the back of the book, the glossary defines key words and phrases that are related to the topic. These words and phrases can be found in the text in colored type.

Comprehension Questions (Fact Check)
Multiple-choice questions help readers self-check to make sure they understand what they read.

Index
Located at the back of the book, the index is an alphabetical list of topics and the page numbers where they can be found.

With a little help and guidance, your reader will be on their way to enjoying and learning from nonfiction books.

Mitchell Lane
PUBLISHERS

mitchelllanepub.com

2001 SW 31st Avenue
Hallandale, FL 33009

First Edition, 2027.
Author: Kim Thompson
Designer: Rhea Magaro

Series: Indigenous American Cultures
Title: Celebrating the Abenaki / by Kim Thompson
Hallandale, FL : Mitchell Lane Publishers, [2027]

Library bound ISBN: 979-8-89260-914-2
Paperback ISBN: 979-8-90145-065-9
eBook ISBN: 979-8-90145-024-6

Library of Congress
Control Number: 2026930178

PHOTO CREDITS
Alamy: Ellen McKnight, 1; ZUMA Press, Inc., 1; George Burba, 1; nobleIMAGES, 5; The Picture Art Collection, 6; piemags, 7; Pictorial Press Ltd, 8; Chuck Nacke, 9; Everett Collection Historical, 9; Erin Paul Donovan, 13; Hemis, 16; FORGET Patrick, 18; Historic Images, 18; gary corbett, 19; megapress images, 19; icpix_can, 20; Hemis, 21; Mario Beauregard Beaustock, 22; Michael Wheatley, 23; Alpha Stock, 24; Miro Vrlik Photography, 24; Maggie Sully, 25; Randy Duchaine, 27; Military Collection, 28; Dreamstime: Micheb 15; Public Domain: Library of Congress, 11; National Archives, 14; Wikipedia, 23, 26; Shutterstock: Juli Fair, 1; MH Anderson Photography, 11; Chantel Dopp, 12; slowmotiongli, 17; Juli Fair, 29;

CONTENTS

AN ABENAKI CONNECTION

Have you ever looked at something in nature and imagined you saw a face? If so, you have something in common with the Abenaki. Thousands of years ago, these **Indigenous** people lived on land that would become New Hampshire.

Up in the mountains, they saw a rock formation they called Great Stone Face. They said the face belonged to an Abenaki man named Nis Kizos. His girlfriend left on a voyage, but she soon died from illness. Nis Kizos did not know. He waited on the mountaintop for his love to return. He waited so long that his face turned to stone.

Culture Close-Up

The rock formation was commonly known as the Old Man of the Mountain. In 2003, it collapsed. Many people in New Hampshire were sad. Some Abenaki were happy. They said Nis Kizos could finally join his girlfriend in heaven.

ABENAKI HISTORY

Abenaki means "toward the dawn." The sun rises in the east, and Abenaki people have always lived in the northeastern part of North America. Long ago, their homes stretched across lands that are now New York, New Hampshire, Vermont, Maine, and Quebec, Canada.

Culture Close-Up

Around 1680, five tribes joined together for protection from neighboring tribes. They formed the Wabanaki **Confederacy**. It includes the Abenaki, Passamaquoddy, Penobscot, Mi'kmaq, and Maliseet peoples.

The Abenaki word Ndakinna *means "our land."*

Ancient Abenaki lived in small groups. In different seasons, they moved to places where food was plentiful. They fished and searched for oysters and lobsters. They hunted for bears, deer, and moose. They also gathered wild foods and planted crops.

In the 1500s and 1600s, Europeans began coming to Abenaki lands. They brought **smallpox** and other diseases. Many Abenaki died. Those that remained traded furs and **pelts** with Europeans to get tools, beads, and other goods.

When the English and French were at war, the Abenaki helped the French. Many lost their lives in battle.

Some Abenaki settled in Quebec, Canada. Those who stayed in America lost their land. Today, there are thousands of Abenaki **descendants** in Canada and the United States.

Culture Close-Up

The government of Canada recognizes the Abenaki as an official tribe. The government of the U.S. does not. Many Abenaki are working to change this.

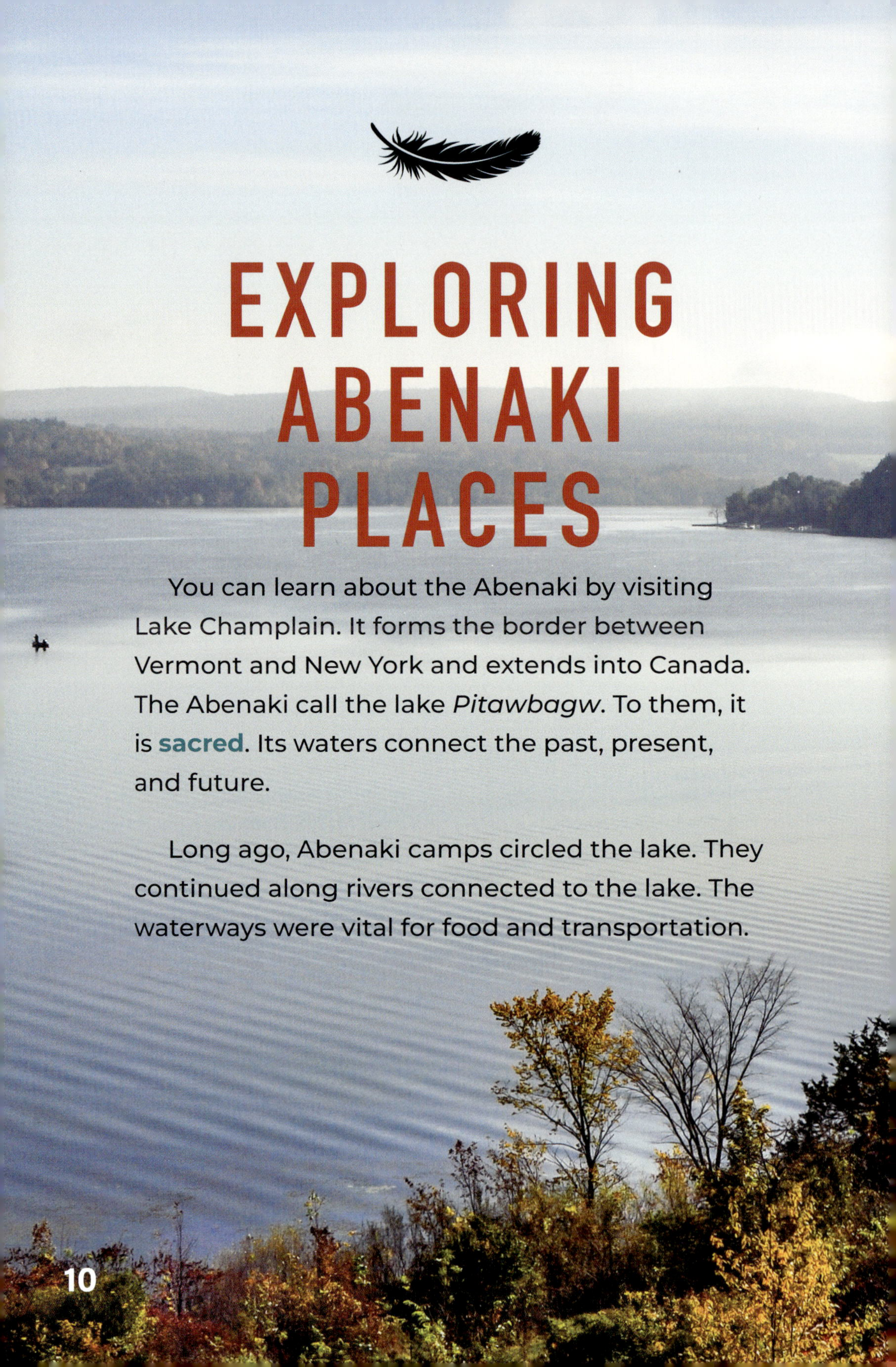

EXPLORING ABENAKI PLACES

You can learn about the Abenaki by visiting Lake Champlain. It forms the border between Vermont and New York and extends into Canada. The Abenaki call the lake *Pitawbagw*. To them, it is **sacred**. Its waters connect the past, present, and future.

Long ago, Abenaki camps circled the lake. They continued along rivers connected to the lake. The waterways were vital for food and transportation.

Culture Close-Up

An Abenaki story tells how Lake Champlain was created by a character named Oodzee-hozo. Afterward, he changed himself into a tiny island now known as Rock Dunder.

You can visit Great Bay in New Hampshire. This **estuary** rises and falls with the ocean tides. It is home to many birds, fish, clams, seals, and other animals. It was an important source of food for Abenaki people.

At the Great Bay Discovery Center, you can learn about this unique environment. You can visit a recreated Native American camp. There is a traditional house called a **wigwam**. It is made from a wood frame covered with bark from birch trees.

An Abenaki village might have had dozens of wigwams. Inside each was a firepit surrounded by raised platforms for sleeping.

ABENAKI LANGUAGES

Eastern Abenaki and Western Abenaki are two languages in a family of languages called Algonquian. Languages in this family are spoken by Indigenous tribes as far north as Canada, as far south as North Carolina, and as far west as the Rocky Mountains.

Not many people speak Abenaki languages. Some groups are trying to change that. They offer online classes and videos. In 2025, the *Nulhegan Abenaki Dictionary* went on sale.

This sign is in Abenaki, French, and English.

Culture Close-Up

Practice these Western Abenaki words.
kwai (hello)
kchi wliwni (great thanks)
tolba (turtle)
awasos (bear)
maskwaimozi (white birch)

HONORING ABENAKI TRADITIONS

Abenaki people have a rich storytelling tradition. Long ago, stories were told aloud and passed down from parents to children. They were often shared to teach lessons.

One story is about Azeban the raccoon. He heard a loud waterfall, but he thought he could yell even louder. He got closer and closer to the waterfall, trying to outshout it. Then, he got a little too close. The waterfall swept him away. What lesson do you think this story teaches?

Abenaki people still like stories. Today, some tell them in modern ways. Kim O'Bomsawin is a writer and movie director. Her films are about the lives of Indigenous people.

Long ago, Abenaki people used what they found in nature to make beautiful and useful objects. They made watertight canoes from birch bark. They used ash wood and sweetgrass to make baskets. Some baskets were used to trap fish.

Wood from ash trees splits easily into flexible strips for basket weaving. Naturally waterproof birch bark is great for building canoes.

Today, Abenaki artists continue these traditions. They build canoes in the old way. They weave natural materials by hand to create baskets that honor their culture.

Culture Close-Up

Many Abenaki people are still good at catching fish. Some enter Indigenous fishing competitions held in Quebec, Canada, and other places.

Abenaki artists have always made totem poles. The towering sculptures are carved from tree trunks. They represent legends, goals, and **values**.

Modern Abenaki artists use modern tools. But they carve the faces of animals and other traditional symbols that are important to their people.

Culture Close-Up

Animals shown on totem poles symbolize important ideas.

Eagle: Sits atop the world, providing a connection to the Creator

Bear: Represents medicine, power, and protection

Beaver: Represents hard work and creativity

Turtle: Represents Earth and the land

ABENAKI CELEBRATIONS

The five tribes that make up the Wabanaki Confederacy call themselves "People of the Dawnland." They often have gatherings. One tribe hosts the others.

Events may include sunrise ceremonies, talking circles, and sacred fires. There is often drumming and dancing.

Mimi O'Bonsawin

Mali Obomsawin

Culture Close-Up

Modern artists such as Mimi O'Bonsawin and Mali Obomsawin keep Abenaki music traditions alive.

In late summer, the Abenaki celebrate the Green Corn Festival. It includes singing, dancing, and prayers. People give thanks for the corn ripening in the fields. They celebrate that there will soon be food to harvest.

Culture Close-Up

Long before Europeans arrived in North America, Abenaki people harvested sap from maple trees in the early spring. They boiled it to make sweet syrup.

Raising the three plants together produced more food compared to planting them separately.

Like other North American tribes, the Abenaki traditionally planted three garden crops together. They were known as the "three sisters." Bean plants improved the soil. They climbed up the tall corn plants. The large leaves of squash plants held moisture close to the ground and kept weeds from sprouting.

FAMOUS FACES

The Battle of Pequawket broke out in 1725. British soldiers attacked an Abenaki village. Chief Paugus led the people in fighting back to defend their land. He died in battle. A mountain in New Hampshire is named after him.

Chief Paugus was shot while defending land that became part of Maine.

Culture Close-Up

Michelle O'Bonsawin is the first Indigenous person to serve as justice on Canada's Supreme Court. She was appointed in 2022.

Wabanaki Confederacy member Mary Pelagie Nicola was a healer and medicine woman. She was born in Maine in 1775. She came to be known as Molly Molasses.

LESSONS FROM THE ABENAKI

The ancient Abenaki lived in harmony with the water and the land. They used natural resources wisely. They relied on their neighbors for strength.

Modern Abenaki people lead ordinary modern lives. But they remember their past and celebrate their **heritage**. Their traditions teach important lessons about honoring nature and community.

GLOSSARY

Confederacy (kuhn-FED-ur-uh-see): a union of groups that join together for a common purpose

descendants (di-SEN-duhnts): your children, their children, and so on into the future; people descended from an ancestor

estuary (ES-choo-er-ee): the wide part of a river where it joins the ocean

heritage (HER-i-tij): traditions and beliefs that people consider to be an important part of their history

Indigenous (in-DI-juh-nuhs): the earliest known inhabitants of a place

pelts (pelts): animal skins

sacred (SAY-krid): holy, very important, and deserving of great respect

smallpox (SMAWL-pahks): a very contagious disease that causes a rash, high fever, and blisters

values (VAL-yooz): beliefs and principles that are important to you

wigwam (WIG-wahm): a hut made of poles and covered with bark or animal skins; the traditional home of Abenaki people

FACT CHECK

1. ________ is sacred to the Abenaki.

   A. Quebec B. Lake Champlain C. The raccoon

2. Nis Kizos was ________.

   A. an eagle B. a chief C. an Abenaki man

3. *Abenaki* means _______.

   A. "toward the dawn" B. "sacred fire" C. "confederacy"

4. Long ago, the Abenaki made _______.

   A. buffalo hides and maple syrup

   B. canoes and wigwams

   C. horse saddles and totem poles

Answers: 1. B, 2. C, 3. A, 4. B

FURTHER READING

Greenlaw, Suzanne, and Gabriel Frey. *The First Blade of Sweetgrass.* Tilbury House Publishers, 2021.

O'Brien, Cynthia. *Encyclopedia of American Indian History and Culture*. National Geographic Kids, 2019.

ON THE INTERNET

National Park Service: Acadia: Wabanaki Nations
nps.gov/acad/learn/historyculture/wabanaki.htm
Learn about the Indigenous history of Acadia National Park in Maine.

The Canadian Encyclopedia: Abenaki
thecanadianencyclopedia.ca/en/article/abenaki
Learn facts about the Abenaki people and watch videos that feature their music, stories, and more.

World History: History and Culture of the Abenaki Tribe
youtube.com/watch?v=F4l-T1rOO8s
Watch a detailed history of the tribe and see pictures of Abenaki people through the years.

INDEX

ABOUT THE AUTHOR

Kim Thompson has written more than one hundred books for young readers. She is a fan of American history and loves digging deep to explore stories from the past. Kim thinks it's important to remember ancestors and keep cultural traditions alive. She's grateful for the privilege and adventure of writing this book.